THE HIGH SHELF

The High Shelf

Nadia Colburn

THE WORD WORKS
WASHINGTON, D.C.

THE WORD WORKS
P.O. Box 42164
Washington, D.C. 20015
editor@wordworksbooks.org

Cover art:
"Wooded Landscape with Merrymakers in a Cart Landschap"
by Hobbema, Rijksmuseum, Amsterdam
Cover design: Susan Pearce
Author photograph: Eric Colburn

LCCN: 2019930536
ISBN: 978-1-944585-36-5

Acknowledgments

I would like to thank the editors of the following journals for publishing some of these poems, sometimes in earlier versions.

American Letters & Commentary: "Protection"
American Poetry Review: "Pregnancy," "The Colors of Arrival," "The Natural World"
Barrow Street: "Survival"
Boston Review: "Into Time"
Colorado Review: "History"
Conjunctions: "What May Be Enough," "The Physical World," "Weightlessness," "A Walk in the Country," "What Nature Cannot Make"
Denver Quarterly: "Continuity," "The Lost Key"
The Kenyon Review: "Morning," "Happiness," "Nothing We Say Is Ever the Soul," "Speaking to a Friend Who Speaks of Suicide"
Lyric: "(Pregnancy)," "All," "Story"
New Orleans Review: "Explanation of the World"
The Poker: "The World's Mirror," "On Clarity," "A Lot, but Not Infinite"
Prairie Schooner: "Notes Toward an Autobiography"
Verse Daily: "(Pregnancy)"
Volt: "Thus"

Contents

ও

ও

For Eric, Gabriel and Simone, who are my lights.

What happened? The stone stepped from the mountain.
Who awakened? You and I.

—Paul Celan
(trans. John Felstiner)

Into Time

Any moment, the red door.

Then, the leaves,
the many leaves, all yellow now,
they are so thin, I think I can feel them
ready to fall.
One breeze, and you:
there, walking
or standing, alone—

What, what do we not become?

Plenitude/Pregnancy

i

The rock that stands on the hill of stone.

The blade that grows between stone.

My self that might be:

At night, in bed, the body relaxes, not lonely. And then, in the long light, stretches first the legs, then the arms—

ii

As the golden cup of emptiness:

      Inside, little legs kicking up against my side,
your little rump now by my navel—

The stones of the hillside
have been gathered into walls, stripes
along the hillside's middle towards which the sheep,
their legs hobbled close together, walk, eager for shade—

the world into which you will come
is a waiting bowl: hear the high echo:

iii

So everywhere, anticipation.

Now I make ready
the tight constraint
            as subject from subject
        leading to verb:

iv

The view of the land.

    The light that changes.

The reversed hollow of the hill
made of likenesses even in difference:

      Far off,
           thistle like thirst.

      Rock like a name
           called out in the dark.

A single tree blown against a wall.

v

In the fluid dark
what do you taste?

       What do you
hear?

The internal the external,
that cannot be separated—

mother to mother to daughter,
passed on. Like a belief
no longer believed, but not yet entirely abandoned:

       the mushrooms of the hills that ward off fever,
       the leaf that, mixed with water, requites desire—the remedy,

taken by mouth, the knowledge, misplaced

in an older country, no longer home.

vi

Then caught in it.

    The waters whip in the same direction,
    then widen out.

        (Water like silence.
        Water like water, a language
        not foreign, not my own.)

    And we, at center, in its tight hold—

vii

Across the terraced hills, more terraces.
The olives the only green, and the spindly broom
with its bright yellow blossoms:
the land made to support them;
the donkeys, at evening, carrying water.

And below, the aquamarine of the sea, now smooth as glass,
that brings back,
open mouthed, black plastic bags.

      O: little one: all this that is not mine
to give you,   what will I give you?

viii

Their leaves a thick, dark, unguent green, their fruit too dry to eat, the figtrees brush all night, one against the other, in the breeze.

Sound like the sound of rain in our own country.

When you are born, may I recognize

the unseen in my arms—

ix

Came into the world.

At center, a silence; activity a cry
      too high to hear; a rent in the sky,
a single cloud.

      Then will come—

Continuity

The sky looks like something unspeakable about to be said. Then doesn't say it. In the world, look how many things are in it. And we, like prairie dogs that make it through the burning.

Last year the trees on the hill in the forest were trees until they weren't. They gave in for three months straight. 50,000 acres taken by this year's weeds from the fire-blackened earth.

Elsewhere, always in the same place: geese. White geese. One day, I stopped and counted: thirty-three.

How life imitates the grace of thought.

The next day, they were still there in the water. Though all along the path their white feathers were strewn. White, white as the sky is today.

In my thoughts, the geese never leave the water. The prairie dogs come up in the first dawn among the weeds that grow from the burned down forest. The smallest girl runs singing through the grasses left unmown at the end of the season.

In my thoughts, what isn't there counts.

ও

The Natural World

It was like waking up one day no longer able to carry a tune.

The little chicks trailing behind their mother searching for food. The hummingbird coming, once, twice, to the bougainvillea vine. The children in the water laughing, feeling the sun on their faces, their arms. The waves showing their white tips, claiming a space, becoming undone.

Three starfish lie on a blanket. Music from a boat that heads to the pleasure island charges the air and is changed: the beat louder, austere, words lost to the wind.

Yes, certainly we will destroy ourselves.

Reading the Newspaper by the Open Window

The world that is alone in its beauty

with no consolation—

the black walnut tree
the double-oleander

the goats, always-hungry—

Who hasn't been seduced?

Who is the wonderful me of happiness?

Of forgetfulness,
of horror,
that must be a part?

As if "all"
were a word in another language.

Now no one speaks.

A Lot, but Not Infinite

The world was imperative.

In all the reaches and very close:
people: huddled,

> for the price of oil,
> for a stone—

So many, so many, each one:

one: numberless:

Someone Goes Hungry

Stomach distended for grain; grain gone to rot.

      Need and the given?

      (All the time: I: trying to rearrange.)

Red geraniums out the window;

                      window's solid frame.

Given

(King Island Emu
Mariana Mallard
Pink-headed Duck
Labrador Duck
New Zealand Quail
Double-Banded Argus
Hawkin's Rail
Red Rail
Red-Throated Wood Rail
White-Winged Sandpiper
Eskimo Curlew
Colombian Grebe
Bermuda Night Heron
Ascension Night Heron
New Zealand Little Bittern
Small St Helena Petrel
Large St Helena Petrel
St Helena Dove
Passenger Pigeon
Silvery Pigeon
Mauritius Blue Pigeon
Rodriguez Gray Pigeon
Bonin Woodpigeon
Sulu Bleeding-heart
Black-Fronted Parakeet
Society Parakeet
Paradise Parrot
Night Parrot
Cuban Red Macaw

Cuban Kite
Laughing Owl
Alfaro's Hummingbird
Imperial Woodpecker
Brace's Emerald
Gould's Emerald
Bush Wren
Red Sea Swallow
White-eyed River Martin
Rueck's Blue Flycatcher
Bay Starling
Mysterious Starling
Black-lored Waxbill)

Whose songs we do not hear.

The Feeling of Trying to Express
the Feeling I Can't Even Name

We assembled it. We made the corners tight, a box

that might hold all of us—

        safe

from everything we wanted to escape and creating

        the idea of escape itself.

What Nature Cannot Make

i

Line–touching–line–touching–line–touching–line.
Four points at the four corners.
Where nothing penetrates.

ii

Closed off (as not even the deepest forest in the most lush days
        of summer,
as not even the edge of the rock-lined lake)
closed off with intent (as not even the cat who cleans herself,
who walks so assuredly along the edge of the balcony,
who tilts back her ears at the call of the cardinal—leaps—
as not even she, with her wise, her elegant ways, would, of her
        own, trace—)

iii

Nor would the sky trace:
not even along the field's horizon.
So everywhere in nature: the inescapable escape—
the branches' thin delicate fingers reaching out to embrace
the air that everywhere, everywhere, once touched, is away.

iv

But with what only the human can make,
I enter, then re-enter.
Then shut the door to this well-ordered space
into which I fold first one limb
and then another, then the four-chambered heart
in the space that might be contained, held in place
by wood that has been sanded and planed,
nailed together with little nails that do not break—

Weightlessness

In the box, there was no beginning and no end, but an openness stopped on all sides by the edges. We built it with wood and painted it. And all along there was the future. Which had no one direction. And which, in the box, would never arrive at any one particular. See? Things as they are. The questions we do not ask.

Survival

There in the painted box, the white coloring the white,
and the white made to look antique. The layers layered up
for the mornings, the coming back.

And many things: a doll: a shell: a window bar: I don't
know how to say this properly, I said. I think the world is
a box with a mirror. I think the many silver things.

The mind a white slate: over and over:
the four corners: touching up.

The I, the I. The you, the I. So close.

A Walk

And I came to the one that was the body. And I came
to the door that was painted white. And I let myself in.
In through the light. In through the small occasion. The
mouth. The eyes. And settled. And I tried to settle.

There: I: I. And sometimes I, a stone. And over the stone,
another stone,
and above the stones, the sky.

Namelessness

In the box I put the body. There were no words
for what had happened.

Outside, all the other boxes. In some, no movement
at all. In some, dancing.

The color like a deep blue lake reflecting the color
of sky: who could say which was original, which the interior,
which the exterior.

Or like the color of the sky at dusk opposite the setting sun:
all silver and the lake beneath all silver: as if something were
          about to happen
or had only just occurred.

Trying Again

A hand in the dark.
A body on the body. On my body.
In the box.
Where time stops.

Here

And, suddenly, like snow: the everywhere: the fear.

Or not fear, but the sound, in the heart's engine, caught,
                                                    out of range.

The Colors of Arrival (*after Mark Rothko*)

And the red. Then the red that would fit around the blue.
And the blue into the red. Then lines among.

Did I think? Did I think differently?

When I was in my childhood. (The small purple
inbetween.) And still the boxes. The things that
keep. Inside and inside. Blue a deeper blue. An
almost black.

When it is named. When I step

                        beyond the frame.

The Physical World (*after Joseph Cornell*)

There was the opposite house, not lit by sun, and the trees all dead-like, cut by the frame. And we were lying there trying to keep ourselves. Trying to keep the other.

And the other trying to keep the other that was just the same, with some little variation. And the brown shingle. And the brown shingle next to it.

The world in-latched. Of-itself made. And the boxes. The little boxes.

Each one just the same, with some little modulation. And in the boxes little partitions. And in the partitions, littler partitions.

And there, in one, a bird.

What May Be Enough

I was giving myself over to work.

The certain requirements. The way one space fit inside another.

And I was giving myself over to the small spaces no-
between: with the words that were simple. Seamless.
That all winter was wintering. And not the questions.
And when the words came: O Land of the very-seen:
                    alive and green: how even the hills were
                    conspirators.

The World

And call it home, and call it very own, now, one instant.
Like light on the water. When we are our own.

৶

Pregnancy

Imagine laundry on a laundry line.

Attached at two points, a white sheet hangs, easily, in air.

It mirrors the white of the sky that, because it is laundry day,
    looks clean, not threatening rain.

This is one scenario.

The sheet dominates, undoing the meaning of sky.

*

In another, the sheet on the line slaps furiously as a white sail on
    a sinking boat at sea.

Now the sheet is secondary.

Though it dominates, it dominates for something else.

Nothingness, because it believes itself the source of meaning,
    accepts the work the sheet does for it.

It wants us to think that the wind, because we cannot see it,
    symbolizes erasure.

It wants us to think into every scene some metaphoric meaning,
    with itself at center.

The sky holds back.

It takes on the look of the dead sailor, of the submersion of hope
    in the certainty of dark water.

Out in the backyard, the sheet becomes a shroud. Perhaps.

*

On laundry day, it is easy to see force.

And to see a fine, clean force in futility.

For on laundry day, if everything looks clean, then everything
looks as it should be.

See how what can't be seen takes the objects of this world and
hurls them about themselves?

The sheet sags, comes back, dancing in the colorless light.

Every inch of its surface touched by the colorless light.

*

We sit by the picture window.

Something's about to disappear.

Something's about to take form.

(Pregnancy)

I will not be scared, I said,

take of me, take of me—begin:

And like a tree. And like a tree

its arms outspread.

That the birds fly up to it.

And like the peeling bark. The twigs.

The dead leaves in the nest—

that something comes: that something comes

and takes my body: that what passes through it

can become—

Explanation of the World

It was a shelf—

a high shelf—

and the boxes, spaced: just   so

each one apart from the other.

      Where was the wall?

Above: firmaments
firmaments: below

Where were the supports?

      The shelf decorated with little shells
      and trees and an orange circle

      and from far, from far off,
the sound of the sea.

At the Horizon

Something settles.

As in the body, the body.

Its incessant ticking like the sound of water up

against the shore, against the shore and the surface never changed.

Where we made holes. Where we made spaces for the soul

to fit into. Where sand comes back

to touch sand. As one day

everything may be

our home.

The Lost Key

Might there be another entryway? Red with a black handle? The holes where the squirrels burrowed in the fall? The stashes of seeds beneath the cellar?

Everywhere windows. Light coming through. Streaks of red across the stone floor. The arms outstretched.

The self climbs up, laboriously, to where it had once jumped down so easily. That I might once again forget to check the lock, that I forget to bolt it, that I no longer need to secure the smallest passageway—

History

The mountain is the mountain's own
mountain. And all the foreign leaves on the forest
bed: red, red:

What will we do
with our souls? Where will we
lay them?

The workmen go about their business,
nails to the boards to build the stairs.

While over itself,
the world folds upon the world:
wind on wind
up the high mountains.

Protection

Yes. I will undo

the grief all over
        that is only wasted; my little selves

all lined up, their fine hard shells, green to the sun,
like copper masks,
              reflecting back.

Necessary/Song

What is the world
     that we be in it?

A catbird flies from the garbage can, a yellow twine in her mouth.

She disappears into the eaves of the house, flies out, mouth empty.

Speaking to a Friend Who Speaks of Suicide

I lower my voice,
       my child playing in the little house, putting in the father,
taking the father out from the bath in his clothes.

And on the other side of the window, across the street, in the
       twilight, wet with rain,

                           the bearing forsythia.

Notes Toward an Autobiography

Quick, quick:
ripples in the water,
geese playing in the bracken,
light that lifts with the wind-blown leaf—

What is the occasion
but matter taking the form of what's been
missing?

That it attach to itself
belief. Then let me—

me, too, be occasion.

෧

Story

On little feet, you run
into the room, holding hands.

The sun is up.
You have discovered, with daddy,
gray and black and white pebbles that you put
into the green pail.

You look up at me. You take one pebble
out from the pail, then another.

This is enough.

Happiness

Wherever I looked something opened.

In the tree, a hole where the squirrel, all fall, brought its nuts.

Amid the sidewalk, the little blades of grass, still strong after the
first snow.

Inside my house there was my body, nestled by the bodies of the
ones I love.

How had I arrived? This measurable space, the stairs
so narrow that the bed frame needed to be sawed in half?

Or, in the dark, the inhalation the exhalation of what,
always escaping,   always calling me back—

Morning

One by one
or ten by ten
or ten thousand by ten thousand.

Like trees in the ancient forest.

And I with my hammer and nails.
With my brush and this new white paint:

so that in the painted box I too become not symbol,
not refuge, not emptiness,
but the unopposed, unopposable backdrop for
everything, even for this one red flower in the low grass
whose symmetry around its center we might almost call
happiness.

Nothing We Say Is Ever the Soul

Walking through the park we imagine
        our children
        coming into the room, letting the door close,
        a vase of tulips
        placed that morning on the kitchen counter.

See, see yourself
in the bare branching larch.

The World's Mirror

Nearby long,
cold days; sky
like water; earth like trees.

       Yellow berries the bear
walks by. Deer still
uninjured, still unafraid.

The mind imagines itself gone:
steps back, comes closer:

      there:

up high, one last leaf
moving,
as if of its own.

Time Box

Certainly, the immortal soul:
the light on the whitewashed wall so glaring.

Now and now and now:

On the floor, you and our child learning to spell
the names of the ones we love
and the flower, with its delicate stem, the leaf and the leaf and
      the petals
fanning out.

On Clarity

Because: the water in the pond is deepest.

Because: the land sinks quickly from the shore.

    : the dirt along the shore is porous.

Because: underneath cold springs,

run-off from the mountains

    (tall mountains meeting snow).

Because whole networks of passageways:

(Because)

       the rocks at bottom seem through the ripples of water to
             be moving below and
       the pebbles and the fine sand, shifting of their own weight

when all the time: from above

    the light: Without which there would be

none.

Second Season

In time, fear wasn't necessary.

I thought of other things.

Crocuses refound beneath the melting snow.

Piles of twigs behind the neighbor's fence given to bloom: bright
gold in a shadowless spot.

Me again.

And there was this dislocation.

Still trying to keep up, not to be jumped beyond, mind kept saying—

kept saying—oh

my little numberless and forced to fit into just one

kept saying—among the one and the many is what

all? While still, the sun on the snow—like the thought of death

that when it comes, comes naturally: that we all must bring

ourselves with ourselves

completely.

Now

Not the box.

Not the high shelf.

But the breath, leaving, coming back.

I lived in the suspension, caught by what I did not know.

Now, summer comes again: again the heat of the sun, again
the children's voices rising from the sprinklers in the park.

Everything I wanted to say is taken up in their voices
                                        and dissipates.

A squirrel comes down the fence and rummages in the basil, eats
        one leaf, then
another and runs back up the tree where it has its nest, high in
        the branches—

        neither caught nor unsupported.

            And tomorrow?

Tomorrow, that the squirrel knows how to gather for, gathering
        not too much
nor too little, tomorrow, that the squirrel does not even try
                                        to name:

The Open Page

i

Imagine three lemons.
Paint the lemons as many times as you can.

ii

Lemon one: the body. Lemon two: the soul.   Lemon three: the intellect.
Lemon one: the soul. Lemon two: the intellect.   Lemon three: the body.
Lemon one: the body. Lemon two: the body.   Lemon three—

iii

And yet, the lemons are as they are:
on a table,
on a chair,
or rolling, one after another,
to the dirt-covered floor, where a dog comes in and smells them.

iv

What, then, is the limit?
        Perhaps one lemon is slightly smaller than the others.
Or one looks a bit like a lime.
            (The tender green at its swollen center.)

And one, perhaps the same, with a piece of its stem attached to itself:
a little dark knob pointing out.

v

Then the fruitbearing tree. And I, reaching up to pluck the lemons
from the fruitbearing tree.
Where is my youth? What, when I reach up, am I forgetting, this time?

The wind in the grass behind me? The staring, omnipotent sun?

vi

And the urgency (the taste
that makes the mouth pucker and then crave more).
To have said that the self is multiple and complete.

To paint as I might sit down beneath a tree:
to see the self as distinct,
a series of finite solutions to a problem.

vii

a) Bring the brush to the page:
b) Take the physical world:

viii

Or any citrus: an orange, a grapefruit.
                          Or three smooth, white eggs.
The slight variation in the color of white:
what is added to the absence.

From such abundance, three objects small enough to hold: touch:
carry them, alone, up the mountainside, and rest by the rocks, by
        the goats,
                          feeling in your hand their own warmth.

ix

Yet, how to show, with this borrowed brush,
        this foreign viscous paint,
the vigor? On the branch, alive, growing

and then: the object, fully other, like a stone,
        carrying only the heat
of something other, borrowed, not its own.

x

I, trying to piece together some story, placing one lemon here, another:

xi

Until it gets easier:

I look away: everything is distinct:
the self falls out of the picture—
and the lemon, suspended, in mid-air, with the hand elsewhere,
and no floor and nothing to rest upon. Only from a distance,
        from far off, the scent of the lemon tree in bloom now,
the small white blossoms,   so many,
        one by one, opening to the bees.

What Can't Be Held

Gone: endlessly, and I
toward the future, like a sailboat to wind, like wind
to the far-no-shore where everything turns—
Like and like and like
to the unlike: as, before me:
what sings.

Afterword

After/Before. To some extent these terms don't matter. It is always both before and after. So I hope that you will go back and re-read these poems—read them in order, read them out of order, in your own order.

Nonetheless: some of these poems were written before and some were written after—before and after any number of destructions and wonders—environmental, political, personal. And before and after recovering the precipitous memories of an early childhood trauma that my body remembered but my mind did not.

We live with a multiplicity of meaning and trauma around us all the time. And both meaning and trauma occur in and to individual bodies, as suffering and healing, too, occur in both body and mind.

These poems were also written before and after the birth of my two children: what for me stopped time, made it start again, what oriented me in space and to my body, and what oriented me to meaning and to love.

The poems walk the fine line of knowing and not-knowing. And their language points both towards what we can and what we cannot say. In the white space of the page is the traumatic unsayable and also the great, ever-opening unsayable that some people call God.

What interests me in this book are not the specifics of the story as much as the fact that normal life is always lived in both the after and the before, personally and historically. As Whitman said, "there is never...more heaven or hell than there is right now." Our challenge is to make space for the beauty of the world and also its suffering even and especially in this fraught moment of earth's history. When so much life is so endangered, it's all the more important that we search again and again for meaning, direction.

So we are always, again and again, finding and losing ourselves as I hope you do in these poems:

before and after—

or neither, at all, but rather here in this moment, just as it is. And from this precarious place, we engage in the human act of making meaning, of making art, of making lives from fullness and from emptiness. Of losing and grieving and creating and celebrating.

My hope is that these poems can help readers hold our fear and our light; that they can help us live with emptiness and still find safety, even without the supports of certainty and without closing ourselves off; that they can open us beyond the dichotomy of self and other, singleness and multiplicity; that they can help us wake up with wonder and with engagement; that they can help us find focus on what matters so that we can act accordingly.

Thank You

I want to thank the many people who supported this book. First, Eric. I don't have words for my thanks and love.

Thank you to Gabriel and Simone; you are for me a testament to the miracle and wonder that the human experience can hold.

To my many friends who read and commented on the poems at various stages, thank you. I apologize for not naming you all here.

To the healers and teachers who have helped me put into language the inexpressible and move beyond fear to a larger horizon that can hold more and be more full of wonder, thank you.

To The Word Works and to everyone there, thank you for giving this book a wonderful home.

Thank you to my poems themselves; these poems have spoken to me with their own wisdom and been an important part of my journey; as I have continued to travel, it is my hope that these poems can stand, independent from me, in their own life, as art does.

And finally, of course and importantly, thank *you*, the readers of this book. My hope is that these poems can be a part of your journey.

About the Author

Nadia Colburn's poetry and prose have been widely published in such places as *American Poetry Review, American Scholar, Kenyon Review, Lion's Roar, The New Yorker, Spirituality & Health Magazine*, and many others. She holds a PhD in English from Columbia University and a BA from Harvard, and is a Kundalini yoga instructor, a serious student of Thich Nhat Hahn, and a committed social justice and environmental activist. She is the founder of Align Your Story classes and coaching for women, and lives in Cambridge, MA, with her husband and two children. To see more and for free meditations and writing prompts visit nadiacolburn.com.

About The Word Works

Since its founding in 1974, The Word Works has steadily published volumes of contemporary poetry and presented public programs. Its imprints include The Washington Prize, The Tenth Gate Prize, The Hilary Tham Capital Collection, and International Editions.

Monthly, The Word Works offers free literary programs in the Chevy Chase, MD, Café Muse series, and each summer it holds free poetry programs in Washington, D.C.'s Rock Creek Park. Word Works programs have included "In the Shadow of the Capitol," a symposium and archival project on the African American intellectual community in segregated Washington, D.C.; the Gunston Arts Center Poetry Series; the Poet Editor panel discussions at The Writer's Center; Master Class workshops; and a writing retreat in Tuscany, Italy.

As a 501(c)3 organization, The Word Works has received awards from the National Endowment for the Arts, the National Endowment for the Humanities, the D.C. Commission on the Arts & Humanities, the Witter Bynner Foundation, Poets & Writers, The Writer's Center, Bell Atlantic, the David G. Taft Foundation, and others, including many generous private patrons.

An archive of artistic and administrative materials in the Washington Writing Archive housed in the George Washington University Gelman Library. It is a member of the Community of Literary Magazines and Presses and its books are distributed by Small Press Distribution.

wordworksbooks.org

Other Word Works Books

Annik Adey-Babinski, *Okay Cool No Smoking Love Pony*
Karren L. Alenier, *Wandering on the Outside*
Karren L. Alenier, ed., *Whose Woods These Are*
Karren L. Alenier & Miles David Moore, eds.,
      Winners: A Retrospective of the Washington Prize
Christopher Bursk, ed., *Cool Fire*
Willa Carroll, *Nerve Chorus*
Grace Cavalieri, *Creature Comforts*
Abby Chew, *A Bear Approaches from the Sky*
Nadia Colburn, *The High Shelf*
Barbara Goldberg, *Berta Broadfoot and Pepin the Short*
Akua Lezli Hope, *Them Gone*
Frannie Lindsay, *If Mercy*
Elaine Maggarrell, *The Madness of Chefs*
Marilyn McCabe, *Glass Factory*
Kevin McLellan, *Ornitheology*
JoAnne McFarland, *Identifying the Body*
Leslie McGrath, *Feminists Are Passing from Our Lives*
Ann Pelletier, *Letter That Never*
Ayaz Pirani, *Happy You Are Here*
W.T. Pfefferle, *My Coolest Shirt*
Jacklyn Potter, Dwaine Rieves, Gary Stein, eds.,
      Cabin Fever: Poets at Joaquin Miller's Cabin
Robert Sargent, *Aspects of a Southern Story*
      & A Woman from Memphis
Miles Waggener, *Superstition Freeway*
Fritz Ward, *Tsunami Diorama*
Camille-Yvette Welsh, *The Four Ugliest Children in Christendom*
Amber West, *Hen & God*
Maceo Whitaker, *Narco Farm*
Nancy White, ed., *Word for Word*

The Washington Prize

The Hilary Tham Capital Collection

International Editions Books

Kajal Ahmad (Alana Marie Levinson-LaBrosse, Mewan Nahro
Said Sofi, and Darya Abdul-Karim Ali Najin, trans.,
with Barbara Goldberg), *Handful of Salt*
Keyne Cheshire (trans.), *Murder at Jagged Rock: A Tragedy by Sophocles*
Jeannette L. Clariond (Curtis Bauer, trans.), *Image of Absence*
Jean Cocteau (Mary-Sherman Willis, trans.), *Grace Notes*
Yoko Danno & James C. Hopkins, *The Blue Door*
Moshe Dor, Barbara Goldberg, Giora Leshem, eds., *The Stones
Remember: Native Israeli Poets*
Moshe Dor (Barbara Goldberg, trans.), *Scorched by the Sun*
Laura Cesarco Eglin (Jesse Lee Kercheval and Catherine Jagoe, trans.),
Reborn in Ink
Vladimir Levchev (Henry Taylor, trans.), *Black Book of the Endangered
Species*

The Tenth Gate Prize

Jennifer Barber, *Works on Paper*, 2015
Lisa Lewis, *Taxonomy of the Missing*, 2017
Brad Richard, *Parasite Kingdom*, 2018
Roger Sedarat, *Haji As Puppet*, 2016
Lisa Sewell, *Impossible Object*, 2014